for **A.**

in hopes you'll find this
and know that it was always yours.

AVA.

ISBN-10: 1542604729
ISBN-13: 978-1542604727

the following are a collection of
days and thoughts
inspired by A.

let love pull you in
and tell me what kind of monster
you become.

day one.

i set fire to the sky
just for you to notice me
and you let the entire world burn.

day two.

let me hold your stare
for longer than three seconds.

let it mean something
when you look at me.

day three.

i think we met by accident
but it felt like something more.

day four.

when i first laid eyes on you,
i knew i would remember you forever.

i knew you would be the bullet
lodged into my brain
refusing to leave.

day five.

'can i help you feel something?'
    you said.

my eyes waited for you to approach me.
waited to know what you meant.

you barely moved.
barely turned towards me
and i could feel you
inside my whole body.

an earthquake.
a tsunami.
a goddamn fucking disaster.

day six.

i woke up.
everything began the same.
   people are hungry.
   people are dying.
   people are alive and not happy.

then,
an implosion.
   today became different.
   today became special.

   today you noticed me
    and i was not the same.

day seven.

is there something here—
   between us?
something we don't have to be afraid of?

something that resembles the truth
   and a storm.

something like the future
   and ends with you
    in my mouth
    on my tongue—
       happy.

day eight.

tell me you feel it too.

tell me you feel
the friction of our energy,
folding into each other
  deep into outer space.

day nine.

turn around
i dare you.

turn around
and fall in love with me
and don't look back.

day ten.

i let you touch my hair
and i felt the inside
of your wrist on my neck
and i felt close to you,
closer than i ever felt to anyone
but i was dying inside.

i didn't know if you felt how i felt
or if you ever will,
and just the small thought
that i was alone in feeling like this
makes it so hard to be alive.

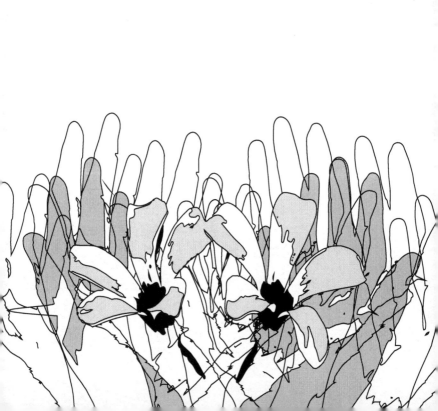

day eleven.

i change the shape of my hands
to something you would want to hold.

day twelve.

you'd take one look at me
and whole pieces of the earth
would break off and fall away

finally leaving me alone with you.

day thirteen.

you need to be careful with me.

i fall in love
and i fall in love forever.

day fourteen.

let me tell you i'm in love with you,
let me tell you that the first thing i do
    when i wake is think of you.

let me be completely honest about this—
    about what you mean to me.

let me take it there
without ruining everything.

day fifteen.

i alter violently
between my love and my sanity.

i do not know how to keep myself
from wanting you.

i do not know how to keep myself
from not going fucking insane
every time you leave.

day sixteen.

my body is intensely aware
of your body next to me.

my body is telling me
to do more.
to not be afraid.
here is your chance at love.
  seize it.

but i lay here
intensely aware
that i am next to you
and you lied down next to me
and i do nothing
but stare at the blank white ceiling
above me.

day seventeen.

and i wonder
when we were alone
in the back of my car,
with your body
pressed up against mine,
and my mouth making
big words and small words,
all meaning *i love you,*

what would have happened
   if i kissed you?

what kind of future love
   would i be living in now?

day eighteen.

i want to sleep
but i keep thinking about you.

and how
you don't love me.

day nineteen.

i keep having this dream
where i keep calling you
and my dream keeps ringing
like i'm inside a bell.
    it rings and rings
    and you never answer,
    and i'm stuck,
    dangling from a swing.
    inside the walls
    of a wishing well.

day twenty.

i don't want to be lonely anymore.

the moon looks so cold and dead-eyed
and the cicadas are still singing their only song.

tonight,
i've come home but
coming home doesn't mean
what it used to mean
when coming home
means coming home to you.

you—
who is here,
who is always here,
but is not free enough
to love me.

day twenty one.

today
i stayed in bed
so i can be alone
with the thought of you
swollen
inside me.

i thought if i stayed still
long enough
you'd see me
and not want to leave.

day twenty two.

i turn on a sad song
and think of you

like i always do.

day twenty three.

i'm not alright.

lay me down.
lay me down
beneath your sky.
beneath your light
and let me breathe you in.

day twenty four.

you, laughing
but not with me.

you, being
but not with me.

what kind of hands must i have for you
to want to hold them?

what kind of voice must i have for you
to hear me?

how much more of me do i need to be?

    how much less than what i am?

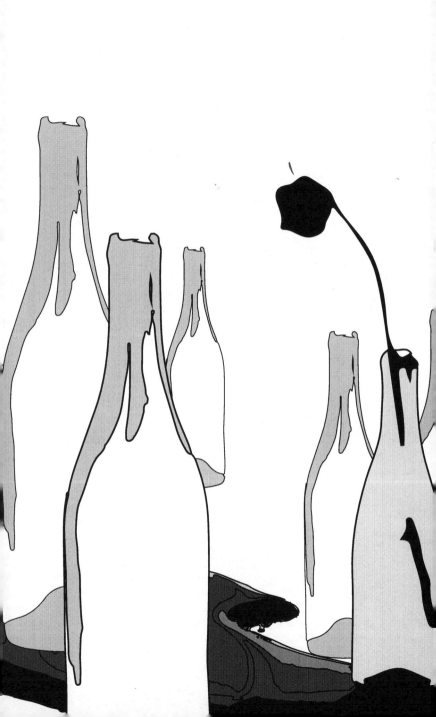

day twenty five.

how many times in the car did i try to reach for you
but reached for the bottle instead?
   11 times.

how many words did i say to you
when all i wanted to say was three?
   542.

i wanted more courage.
i thought i could drink it in, but fear is a monster.
fear is that voice in my head i obey too often.

i looked out the window.
it was night and everything was black. we were alone.
i thought this could be enough for now.
i thought i could live with not wanting more.
   this is enough. i am happy.

some people build their whole lives on a lie.
some people build whole empires protecting them.
   i was with you, but i was alone.
   i was alone except for fear.
   this is enough. i am happy.

day twenty six.

i lied.
i think about you everyday.
i cannot leave a single thought
    without you intervening.

day twenty seven.

there are feelings that exist in me
that do not exist in you,
and i've always had a problem with
inventing things that are not there.

i've created a home inside you,
inside me, for you.

i've created stories that were to exist
in our future.

i've created an idea of you
that you could never live up to,
and all of this has created a hole
that turns everything black
inside of me.

day twenty eight.

last night
the way your eyes held me
through the long green hallway
and into the next room

i can still feel my heart
   in my throat.
i can still feel your eyes
   in my eyes.

how intimate your stare.
how immediate your hold.

day twenty nine.

i think you know what you do to me;
otherwise,
why would you do it?

i can't touch you,
but you can touch me;
i know i shouldn't let you,
but i'm weak.

your beautiful brain,
warm inside my lap.
your beautiful lips,
speaking only to me.

we're alone in this world.
we're happy in this place.
we are where we want to be—

except i can't have you
while you will always have me.

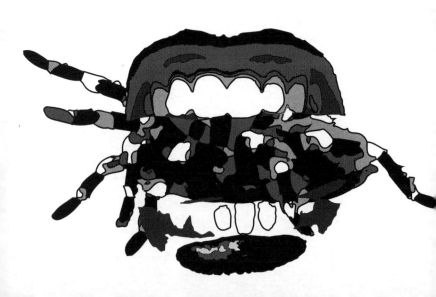

day thirty.

i am trying to write you next to me.
how many times have i wanted this?
how many days and nights since you've left?

how many times have i wanted to feel you
    here—
warm blood and red heat
    beneath my skin.
    beneath my nails.
    between my legs.
    between my teeth.

how long must i wait for you
    when i want you
        now.
        now.
        now.
        now.

day thirty one.

you wear the sky on your skin
and when i breathe you in
        i fly.

day thirty two.

you tell me
  no one writes longing like you.
and hot tea burns my tongue.
hot tea, black and bitter.
last night's whiskey, coming back as revenge.

you ask me
  who are you longing for?
and i think of how much skin will it take
to hold all this pain.
i think of your tongue in my mouth.
i think of your name.

i say nothing.
i say it's just words.
  letters like black hair.
  lies, mountain fresh on my lips.
i love you
        deep in the dark.
i want you
        always on my mind.

forgive me, i said.
i've burned my tongue.

day thirty three.

there is this pull between us.
this science that is
strange and seductive,
heavy with feeling,
thick and layered
like atmosphere.

this energy, so pretty,
we find ourselves
in the middle
in each other.

day thirty four.

we were sitting across each other
over a white tablecloth restaurant.
the sun was setting and
turning the room into gold.
the drinks between us
began to bleed into round grey rings
and you said
the sun is getting into your eyes.
come closer to me.

you motioned me next to you and i hesitated
because i had fallen in love with you long ago
and i was afraid it was just me.

i moved and fell straight into your eyes
and you fell into my mouth
and we no longer cared
if we never came up for air.

day thirty five.

stop thinking.
all the lights are green.
come kiss me.

day thirty six.

i don't know how it goes for anyone else,
but i know that when you speak
   i have to listen.

i have to know what's inside of you.
i have to know why
   i am drawn to you this way.

day thirty seven.

coffee, black
toast, half-eaten
letters, unopened
tobacco, burned
sandalwood hints
a phone, ringing
a song, playing
a bruise, fading
a door, open
a bed, cold

and my mind always goes to you.

day thirty eight.

we light our cigarettes
and pretend they're little stars
dancing to their death in our hands.

you lean in
and you tell me
you want more nights like this.
more nights beating love into our hearts
with me
sitting next to you
and this warm feeling
of being slightly out of our skin
and closer to each other.

day thirty nine.

tension is growing in your fingers.
   it is teeming. it is hot.
   it is a train of beggars,
       full of hands.

you want to touch me.
you want to know what that feels like,
but i keep telling you *not yet.*

i want the waiting to be unbearable.

i want you to want me so badly
that breathing begins to hurt
and loving burns through your skin
       like acid rain.

day forty.

i held you in my mouth like a prayer.

i had to ask god
  if i was enough to keep you here.

day forty one.

i drive my fingers
down your road of skin
and you open yourself up to me.

i rest my hand here
on you
like this,
and you tell me
you feel the entire weight
of the pacific ocean
crashing into your heart.

day forty two.

i wear it well.
you on my skin.
like pearls. like jewels.
like all the things
that love to be as they are
in the sun.
in the morning. in the night.
you on my skin
a tremor. a dance.
like diamonds in moonlight.

your kisses beneath the neck.
your secrets hidden in my right hand.
your left hand, home just beneath the breast.
your love kept locked and safe between my legs.
how you hold me
here.
and here.
and here.
your tongue, the hungry beast i worship.
your mind, the playground i find my childhood
   over and over.
but it's your skin that keeps me.

that stunning pain.
that sweet sorrow.

your skin on my skin.
the new god.
the new religion.

day forty three.

i feel like i've been here before
laying here
watching you
waiting with you like this
in the midday
dark heat
with your back against the sun
and you
preparing to leave.

you look at me before you go.
time has won again.

you look at me
watching you
and you leave

with your taste
still wet on my lips
and your hands
still fresh in my hair.

day forty four.

i love the way
you let me in.

i love the way
you would wrap yourself around me
and how i would feel your heart beat
in between the heat of your thighs.

day forty five.

i love you open mouth
and open legs.

i love you deep and blue
as the ocean that's carved
its soul inside you.

day forty six.

you
sleepyhead.
you
black hair.

you
something beautiful.
something night.

you
warm heart.
you
dark love.

you
something magic.
something bright.

day forty seven.

the sky looked incredible tonight
and i thought of you.

i always think of you
when i shouldn't.

when i am surrounded
    in a crowded room.
when i am touching myself.

when i am alone
and feeling alone
with how i feel.

day forty eight.

i love you if you stay.
i love you if you go.
that will never change for me.

AVA. currently lives in southern california and always has tacos on her mind.

etsy.com/shop/AVApoetry
instagram.com/VAV.AVA
twitter.com/vav__ava

Made in the USA
Middletown, DE
17 October 2017